MINDFULNESS:

HOW TO BE IN THE PRESENT MOMENT EVERYWHERE IN YOUR EVERYDAY LIFE

JANE PETERS

Contents

Introduction

I want to thank you and commend you for opening the book, "Mindfulness: How to be in the present moment everywhere in your everyday life".

Within this book's pages, you'll find out how to live in the moment and be awakened by each experience, as well as meditation.

Many of you are probably wondering about the hype of mindfulness. Despite being around for thousands of years, the closing of 2013 and the beginning of 2014 marked a new surge of research and talk about mindfulness.

Simply because mindfulness is the practice of being immersed in the moment. You are fully aware, focused, and attentive. Mindfulness has been studied by psychotherapists for a long time now, about 4 or 5 decades, because it overlaps with their field and has been found as successful. Mindfulness has been known to reduce stress and help treat disorders such as anxiety, depression, insomnia and in some cases even addiction.

You may not think so now, but I can probably guess that you are busy all of the time. Your nights are too short. Your days are filled with too many tasks. Your caffeine isn't strong enough to turn you into a superhero and more than anything; you wish you had the power to bend time to your will—or at least manipulate time enough so you can have the peace of mind to get through your ever-growing to-do list and find a sense of accomplishment. You wake up thinking about all the things you have to do that day and you go to bed reviewing everything you did do and everything you failed to do.

And just like you, there are so many others out there who are too busy dwelling on the past and worrying about the future, to realize they are living in a moment.

This moment.

It's no wonder depression, anxiety, stress and insomnia are all on the rise. We have all forgotten what it's like to just exist. What it's like to be us, as natural human beings. You have forgotten what it's like to be you. To be alive, sitting in that chair, reading this book, sipping on your coffee or your tea. The smell of your favorite blanket curled up over your feet, the sound the cat makes purring on your lap.

There is no doubt about it; globalization is shrinking this world. Places to go. People to see. Business to attend to. We have lists of lists and apps to help us keep our lists in check. But it shouldn't be shrinking you with it and if you feel like you're shrinking away from the world, then we're just in time.

This book is going to help you recover more than just the moment. It's going to help you recover yourself. And we are going to do that by teaching you how to stay grounded and immersed in the present even when your past feels unfinished and your future feels unclear.

Thank you and I hope that you enjoy reading this book.

PART 1:
Establishing the need for Mindfulness

Chapter I. Life and Distraction

How did you spend your day yesterday? I'm pretty sure you will be able to describe how you got out of bed and carried on with your daily routine, all the way through your hectic schedule until it's time to hunker down again. What I'm not too sure is if you will be able to say "There was some time in the afternoon when I was just sitting around doing nothing" or "I spent a few minutes staring into space when I woke up". Because in all likelihood, you were still doing *something* even during those "idle" times. Perhaps you were checking your Facebook, perhaps you were planning the next out-of-town trip in your head, or perhaps you were recalling that brilliant scene from a movie you just watched. But still, you were doing *something* even in the middle of *nothing*.

Let's confront that question directly. When was the last time you spent a long period of time -- even a few hours would count -- staying still and undisturbed by gadgets, books, friends, food, drinks, worries, problems, or anything of the sort? Now you see just how busy the human brain has become as time passes. People of old had to toil for the whole day just to make sure there's food they could bring to the table. And yet, most of the greatest masters in mindfulness came from those periods. Think -- Buddhist monks, for example. In contrast, people of today have all the comfort of technology -- and yet even a few minutes of absolute nothing can feel very disconcerting.

Come to think of it, there is nothing inherently wrong with spending time on these activities. In fact, these were all meant to be enjoyed. However, it is also useful to understand that these activities all work towards a state of *temporary* "happiness", instead of a lasting sense of calm and peace that is so badly missing from the modern lifestyle. Further, instead of letting you have that calm and peace, these activities all seem to demand them as a payment -- not an outstanding trade-off, if we look closely.

Perhaps the most disconcerting is the fact that we seem to be so addicted to all this. Let's have a little experiment -- put down this book, close your eyes and try sitting still for just one whole minute. Try putting off all those thoughts that come into your mind. Now, how was it? Perhaps you found it relaxing. Or perhaps, you were uneasy, spending that one minute trying to fight off the surge of thought that rushed in. Or perhaps you were squirming, wanting to do *something* -- something that in the end might be of little consequence. (Don't worry about your results for now, though -- we will do this again later with more specific instructions.)

Perhaps the most apt term for all these things is "distraction" -- and a lot of us spend most of our lives moving on from one distraction to another. When we get up, we are distracted by the Facebook posts we missed through the night. When we get to work, we are distracted by the dozen emails waiting in our inbox. When we leave for home (or basically anytime we take a peek at the outside world), we are distracted by the countless advertisements all vying for our attention.

All these distractions tend to push out the more important things playing in our minds, things we don't pay attention to up until all the distracting stimuli are switched off -- such as when we lie awake in bed, trying to sleep but unable to shake off the thoughts of things we should have done (or ought to do). In the end, responding to all the stimuli can leave us even more stressed than before -- and only marginally happier.

In plain words, all of these distractions tend to affect how we concentrate, how we perform, how we react to things -- how we live, in general. But in today's hyperfast lifestyle, we no longer have the option of evading these on a daily basis. Short of being a hermit, we will all have to read emails and check out our Facebook posts at one point. We can all try restricting our responses to these stimuli to, say, just a few minutes a day -- but let's face it: for a vast majority of us, that's impossible to keep up for the long run.

What we need is a way to mitigate the effects these distractions bring into our lives -- a way to turn the tables on the stimuli that keep us hostage.

Chapter II. Enter Mindfulness

Living in our world as it is now, we find that there is no "off" button for most things. We can't resist the winds -- we have to bend or else we break. But hey, we are not simply trees -- we are mobile, sapient beings. It's even better if we can find a way to relate to the winds, studying their properties carefully and working around them -- or with them -- skillfully.

This is the fundamental idea behind mindfulness -- a commonly misunderstood concept.

Mindfulness is an idea that does not require you to change anything. It is not like a martial art that teaches you how to counter your opponents (really, who can counter TV ads?). Instead, it is a science that teaches you to look both within and without, carefully observing, noting, experimenting. If you find that you need to make changes, that is entirely up to you -- it is in no way a requirement.

Perhaps the previous paragraph seems strange to you -- for most of us, the word "mindfulness" evokes images of monks in robes, sitting cross-legged and *meditating* for the better part of the day, while isolated in a mountaintop monastery. The term seems to connote an esoteric idea, something of a lost art that can transform lives when found and put to use.

Well, yes, mindfulness is an art -- but it is not essentially lost. Most of us have our moments of mindfulness, we just don't notice it. Yes, those mountain top monks practice mindfulness, but isolation and a vow of poverty are not requirements in any way. Yes, meditation utilizes mindfulness, but meditation is far from the only way mindfulness can manifest. In fact, you can live the remainder of your days in a state of mindfulness if you choose -- talk about transforming a life!

Chapter III: Why Mindfulness?

It can't help you deflect bullets like Neo in the Matrix; neither can it help you bend the elements like Aang in Avatar. But it can still do wonders to your daily life!

Mindfulness is a stress-buster. In the previous chapter, we discussed all about the negative effects of our modernized lives. What we have are countless hours of stress piled upon stress, and almost no breaks in between. Our minds and bodies are constantly overclocked, and may even be so while asleep! Sometimes, a simple visit to the doctor can help. A few lifestyle changes here and there, some sort of medication, plus some money to pay for the fees, and stress issues might be resolved -- temporarily. Count a few weeks and we're back to saying and doing things we wish we hadn't.

But where do you think the best doctors turn to when their patients won't get better? Therapists, they're who -- those who know and practice mindfulness and can teach them to others. People may be overwhelmed by work or family affairs, and some might be simply seeking for a way out of their boxed regimens. Whatever the reason, mindfulness works against stress and its effects on the body. And you don't even have to shell out money for it!

Mindfulness helps build relationships. Some of

the most stressful things in life are those that make it turn -- the people. Like it or not, we have to deal with them since our relationships can make or break a lot of things. That said, a person who practices mindfulness can help turn even the worst of relationship woes into something better.

When the practice of mindfulness was transplanted to the West from its Oriental origins, it seemed to lose a lot of things. Suddenly, the practice was all about the *self* -- improving oneself presumably in order to put him above others. This might have been inevitable at first, but this way, it has lost much of its meaning.

Let's think of it this way -- when you have problems, it is so easy to mull about it and sulk. This is regardless of the magnitude of your concern. Mundane things can be blown up to such a proportion that we lose sight of the bigger picture (case in point: social media). However, when we are mindful of things such as our problems, we begin to consider things in a more altruistic light. We see how this problem fits into the bigger picture of our surroundings and our relations. Thus, we are less likely to blow things up by taking out frustrations on a colleague or a loved one. And if the issue is with another person, we get to see things in their eyes as well -- an important step in avoiding conflict and healing wounded feelings.

In the end, mindfulness is as much a way to improve one's outlook on others inasmuch as it helps him improve himself.

Mindfulness is realistic. When something is wearing us out, everyone will caution us to avoid it. So what if the thing that wears you down is your daily life? Everyone will tell you to make changes -- changes so substantial that they are hardly realistic. Indeed, making such changes can be no different from dieting -- you try and try to stick to it, but there are times when you "just slip". And like how weight gain comes faster after a failed diet, so does stress strike harder after you know you've failed your mission to change.

So what's the solution? Something realistic -- something that can fit into the daily framework while also being solidly effective.

Mindfulness is your best bet -- it is backed by science and thousands of years of effective practice. Once you understand its principles, you can easily integrate it into your daily life. You don't have to live like a hermit to be a mindful person -- you only need to understand the concepts behind it.

PART 2:
The Components of
Mindfulness

We mentioned earlier that there was a social element to mindfulness (and meditation, by extension) that was lost as the practice was imported to the West. In fact, tradition has it that meditation wasn't usually practiced alone. First, its practitioners didn't usually practice *by themselves*. They were usually in a group -- similar to the modern-day yoga class. Second, it was not practiced *by itself* -- it was always a part of a larger and more holistic system.

Specifically, there are three key aspects to this mind training system. The first part is the *approach* -- the way that one discovers the different dynamics of the human mind, and how it tends to behave. The second is the *practice* -- this includes mindfulness and its big sister meditation. The third is the *integration*, or how the first two fit seamlessly into the fabric of your daily life.

Hold on... What defines mindfulness and meditation, anyway?

We have thrown around the words "mindfulness" and "meditation" for quite some time now, and we have yet to define which is which. If you were to be asked this, perhaps one of the first things to pop into your mind is that "meditation" is what you do when you sit down for long periods of time -- just like in the movies.

Of course this answer is hardly correct -- but it is not completely wrong, either. "Mindfulness" is a state of mind, whose nature and applications we are exploring. It can be practiced at any position, at any activity. However, "meditation" is mindfulness on steroids -- it is when you actually sit down to intensify your mindfulness. It is not necessarily a higher form, but it is more extensive. If mindfulness is running, meditation is like a marathon.

But not everyone can run a marathon on a daily basis, right? In contrast, anyone can run during varying activities. This is why mindfulness can become the efficient and realistic tool we had established it to be.

Now, back on track

So our modern form of mind training is missing two important pieces out of three -- how are we making it work?

The answer is -- we're not really making it work. At least not in the way it was supposed to.

Here's a concrete, real-life example. Most of the people who have tried meditation are being taught to sit still somewhere quiet, and watch out for thoughts that might pop up in their minds. What they do with these thoughts will depend on the person teaching them -- either they "accept" the presence of these thoughts and try to suppress them (accept and suppress do not really belong in the same sentence) or they simply "let it be", allowing the thoughts to run their full course without getting distracted by them.

And of course, the longer the new practitioner sits on

that mat, the more frustrated he gets. Rare is the person who can do either of those things at first. So he is told to try harder -- which will only frustrate him more. The more one tries to suppress thoughts, the more they run amok. Similarly, the more one lets thoughts run while trying not to touch them, the more one is more likely to get distracted.

This is just a manifestation of how unrooted practice turns away would-be practitioners. These people are being asked to meditate without first letting them grasp the nature of mindfulness. While there are some who are successful at doing this, this comes at a price of a lot of unnecessary effort. Also, these people are usually hardly successful at integrating the practice into their daily lives, treating mindfulness and meditation as a sort of mini-retreat when it should have been a part of them all along.

Note that among the three aspects of mindfulness, none is above the other. For the process to work, the practitioner must understand exactly how each one relates to the other two and to the whole. This is the secret of true mindful living.

PART 3:

The Approach

When masters of meditation mention the achievement of a "quiet, empty" mind, they may be sending the wrong message (or maybe it's just the public that's receiving it wrong). Interestingly, the way to that quiet mind is neither through sweeping the thoughts under a mental carpet, nor through letting them run and just letting them be. Instead, the correct approach is in recognizing those thoughts and just "observing" them.

Imagine this scenario. You are in the middle of an open park with lots of people around you. Everyone is doing something, and there is a great deal of noise. It seems like they're all going somewhere, but you can't see them -- someone had placed a blindfold around your eyes.

This is you, in your present state, and the people are the individual thoughts. There are lots of things going on around you, but you may not be seeing them because of a blindfold of distractions, stress, misplaced priorities, etc. They may all be leading somewhere, and you still do not know. You may try following them blindly, but you will eventually get lost.

Now, imagine taking off this blindfold. You will see everyone -- all faces and activities -- distinctly. This is what happens when you first achieve a mindful state -- you are able to see what's going on in a clearer light than before. However, you have been told to recognize each thought and stop it in its tracks -- so you go to the nearest person, "familiarize" yourself with him, then try to stop him from his inexorable movement. Even if you succeed, how much time and effort must you put in to stop everyone?

Or, you may try just standing there, doing nothing, letting everyone pass by you. More people will be coming and going steadily, and your passive presence there is not helping things. Your impulse tells you to do something, but you are resisting that.

As we can see, neither of these two analogies make any real sense as regards to mindfulness. What should you do instead?

Chapter IV: The Mindful Observer

How about this -- imagine removing the blindfold and seeing everyone around you clearly. After assessing the situation, you *move to the side* -- you observe, and try to make sense of what is happening. You are neither an active participant, nor are you a mental statue that the thoughts just pass by. Instead, you are now a mindful observer.

With this new role, you are able to see each and every thought in your mental park in a different light. You can clearly see how they act, and perhaps why they act that way. You will also be able to see where these thoughts are going. From this vantage point, you are more suited to make a decision on what you should be doing next.

This is the mindful state -- a state of constant observation, but not one that is marred with external pressures. It is the act of stepping back from your thoughts and feelings, and watching them from the sidelines. You might slip and reach out to one of these thoughts, but even that is not a taboo. So long as you realize this, you are given the opportunity to go back to your observer's post and resume your watch.

Now, doesn't this sound more enticing than any other technique you have heard before?

Chapter V: "Controlling the Mind"

At one point during all these "step back and watch exercise", you might come to this question: okay, here is me, watching all these thoughts -- but who is doing all the thinking?

Many people who go to conventional mindfulness lessons are taught to "control the mind". We have already seen how this does not work in practice. It is so much that some people attribute the overabundance of thoughts in their mind to the practice of mindfulness itself -- as if the process is making them think more and more!

However, this is not the case. We like to think that we control our minds, and that we choose what we wish to think. Anyone lying awake in bed for the nth hour of the night would know this is not true. Thoughts are autonomous -- oftentimes we do not conjure them, just curate them. We simply skim over them and select which ones should go to the foreground. If you could, wouldn't you have simply blocked out all the disturbing thoughts and lived with all the happy and peaceful ones?

There are many scientific explanations for the origins of thought, but in the study of mindfulness, we are only concerned with the latter part -- the process of passively curating these thoughts. Come to think of it, if we can effectively curate our thoughts, then we would have less reason to be stressed or anxious -- simply because observation and curation are just two of the steps that lead to organization.

The process of curating our thoughts also lends a stillness that is absent from the way we normally think. If you were one of those people in your mental park, then you wouldn't have been able to see the "bigger picture" around you. However, as the observer, you can clearly see everything, including where these thoughts stem from and to where they lead. Ultimately, the mindfulness practitioner will be able to organize these existing thoughts in such a way that more productive thoughts can come in -- in much the same way that a traffic enforcer clears roads to let each vehicle pass though smoothly. This is as close as we can get to "controlling the mind".

Chapter VI: To Do, or Not To Do

We have already established that mindfulness is a practice of giving up control, of stepping back and *not doing*. By now, you should have tried the mind park exercise we had earlier (if not, you should). How easy is it for you to step back and simply watch?

For many of us, it will be difficult to *do* something that is concentrated on *not doing* something. Sure, sitting in one of those mental park benches and watching the people pass by would be fine for the first few minutes -- until suddenly you will find yourself impatiently waiting for some progress or elusive insight. You might end up touching gloves with these thoughts and not letting go, ruining the whole point of the exercise. Or, if you have gone through the entire thing, you might end up with a quieter train of thoughts but still no closer to the mental and emotional stillness you have been searching for.

So let's envision another analogy. Think of a beach -- white sand, lapping waves and all. There are no people, no footprints on the sand. Next, imagine that this beach is your mind -- not the mind with all the thoughts running helter-skelter, but the mind in its base state. How hard this exercise will be for you will depend on how hard you can envision your mind as a blank slate. If it proves difficult, at least try to imagine a time when you feel very happy and relaxed.

Now that you have this beautiful picture, let's try

imagining that beach during summertime -- people everywhere, milling about in confused masses, raking up the sand, leaving heaps of trash near the shores. How does this make you feel? Remember, you are not *on* the beach with these people -- you are the beach itself.

Again, these people are your thoughts. Sometimes there are lots of them, driving you crazy. Sometimes, the number is manageable. The number of people will just reflect your mood or feeling at any given time.

But here's the deal -- in the end, the beach will always be there. The sand, the waves, the sun -- they may be messed up by everything running amok in your mind, but the beach will always be there. The people will leave, and the beach will regain its base state -- just like that picturesque image you had at the start of the exercise. No matter what happens, your mind will always be this beach.

For most of us, the thoughts have been running around so much that we forget how the beach used to look like. When we feel bad, when we have problems, all those people seem all the more obvious and distracting. And yet time will come when we can see the peaceful image again, and how good it would feel!

In a way, mindfulness is also training the mind to see this beach as it is, instead of focusing on the people or trying to keep them in line. In order to avoid distractions while standing back and keeping watch -- in order to avoid *doing* what you should *not* be doing -- you have to keep your attention focused on the mind itself. You have to keep sight of the base state of your mind even as you watch all those thoughts. This is much like shooting a gun down the range -- you have to keep your eyes focused on the sights, even as you view your target.

Chapter VII: Mindfulness and the Wild Horse

Most mindfulness practitioners -- even the masters -- must envy the iconic mountaintop monk. These people have all the time in the world to meditate, and they can tailor every other activity to center around their mindfulness practice. For us living in the world, this isn't always an option.

In fact, one of the more difficult things in the daily practice of mindfulness is how to approach it when you are having a grueling time. Surely, you can't simply walk out in the middle of a high-stakes meeting, just to gain your mindful composure. And even if you can spare a few minutes, you are too tightly strung to effectively ease in. When the mind does not settle into the mindful state as soon as one is used to, the urging of distractions intensifies. Most people fall back into their old ways of attempting to control every thought -- this is a very real temptation you have to be watchful of.

So what does it take to properly approach the practice of mindfulness in the middle of a busy life? Again, let us use an example. Picture a wild horse -- a free spirit used to running over great distances. Imagine trying to catch and tame this horse. It doesn't matter how strong you are -- human muscles are no match for the strength of a horse. If you try to pin him down using brute strength, it will easily overpower you. As experts will tell you, force is never the right way to catch a wild horse.

The mind is like this wild horse -- it is hard to catch it, and impossible to tame it with force. It will overpower your will and slip away. Like a wild horse, however, it can be tamed by first giving it room to move -- lots of room. You can never expect it to sit still just because you want it to. On the same note, you cannot induce the mind to sit still even if you yourself are still as a rock. You will first have to give it time to settle, to relax, to ease into the new state. The next moment is never as important as the current one, so why hurry?

Instead of forcing the mind to sit still at the flick of your wrist, break it in as an expert would a wild horse. Give it all the space it needs to wander as it pleases. And then, slowly, reel it in. Do this gently enough, and neither the wild horse nor your mind will notice the difference. In the end, your mind will reach its state of rest, and you can proceed with your practice.

Chapter VIII: Mindfulness and Emotion

Another hurdle that a mindfulness practitioner will experience is that of emotions. Scientists say that emotions are commonly of chemical (hormonal) origin, and through this, they can deeply affect the state of mind. A strong emotion can throw off or completely ruin your mindful state, to the point that the practice itself may even cause physical discomfort.

Again, this happens to everybody -- even to the masters of mindfulness. We become so attached to the good feelings we have that when an adverse emotion takes its place, try to chase the good feelings floating away. The problem is, the more we try to do this, the more these feelings become elusive.

The problem is that this happens even when there are no bad emotions. As soon as we feel something positive when we begin our mindfulness practice, we try to recreate it during the next. It becomes like a benchmark we chase after, as we seek to recreate something from the past instead of being "in the moment".

This creates a busy atmosphere for the mind. We are trying to regain all the good things, all the while trying to thwart all the bad ones. We are creating both a longing and resistance -- shoving away the room for acceptance. And as we have demonstrated before, acceptance is the key to a peaceful mind.

Sure, you might think -- it's easy to say "let go" of both attachment and resistance. But how? For this, we will be circling back to the linchpin of the entire mindfulness approach -- by being aware.

As awareness grows within the mind, perspective shifts -- you will get a glimpse of this as you read through this book. However, impatience will be a common adversary -- people tend to think that this change in perspective does not happen fast enough.

So here is an exercise that is meant to give you a paradigm shift amidst all these emotions. Imagine sitting down, focusing on your breath, and practicing mindfulness (for now you may settle on the "stepping back" exercises we did earlier). However, imagine that you are not doing this alone -- imagine that you are sitting with people you care about. It could be your friends, family, or significant other.

Now, when a pleasant sensation comes up, imagine yourself sharing all these emotions with others. This does not have to take up much of your attention -- simply imagine that you are handing out the good emotions. Then, when bad thoughts come up, imagine that you are sitting there and feeling the discomfort from the others -- as if you are drawing these ill emotions from the rest of the group.

Unorthodox? Maybe. But this is also a very useful exercise, and a skillful way of working with the mind. It works like this: when a person tries to "hoard" all the pleasant emotions of the mind, then it creates tension in the self. When we envision ourselves giving away the emotion, we remove the tension by taking away its root (note that the root is our hoarding, and not the emotion itself). In the same vein, we always try to get rid of all the bad emotions coming our way. This also creates resistance -- an undue tension. When we imagine that we carry these ill thoughts for others, then we get rid of the root of the tension as well. As a plus, this exercise is a means of practicing altruism.

Chapter IX: "Karma"

The term "karma" does not really play any essential role in the field of mindfulness -- it is more of an accessory than a central concept. However, it can be used to illustrate the next concept of the approach to mindfulness.

"Karma" is often defined by many as "what goes around comes around". It is like a law of reciprocals. It can also be a good way to describe how a practitioner ought to deal with extreme emotions.

In the previous section, we had defined the process of defusing the tension caused by emotions. However, there is another type of emotion that resides within all of us -- that emotion which springs from past faults, problems, etc. It can be a scar of a traumatic past, and it can also stem from a certain regret. This is vastly different from the emotion that comes from the present, and often, these extreme emotions resurface only when our minds are clear. Throughout other times, mental barriers that we create may be able to repress them.

Oftentimes, these emotions are a direct, almost karmic reaction of the things we had done (or had been done to us in the past). Perhaps we took an opportunity for granted -- while such a choice may not have completely affected us, we are stricken with a feeling of regret that stays for a long time. This feeling of regret "comes around" and throws our mindfulness practice off course years later, simply because we are not yet able to deal with it. The repercussions might not have hit us directly, but the feeling of "I could have done something else" can impact us in a way no direct reaction could have. Just like in karma, there is always something that goes around. What more if we are in the epicenter of all the events leading to these long-term repressed emotions?

Now, you might be expecting this chapter to show you how to repress these emotions to a point where they will be permanently chained into a corner of your mind. First thing -- that is impossible. Short of hypnotically reprogramming the brain, there is no way for a person to remove those emotions permanently. The simple reason behind it is that human emotions are like coins -- two opposite sides that may never meet, but will always co-exist. If a man takes away his ability to feel the negative emotions of the past, he will also render himself unable to feel the good emotions stemming from brighter memories.

This does not mean that there is no way to deal with this. But to discuss this, we will have to circle back to the entire point of this chapter -- the correct approach to mindfulness. Many people approach this entire concept as a means to gain "happiness" and comfort as a substitute for whatever they are feeling right now. Simply put, this is not the aim of mindfulness at all. Instead, the practice is a tool to help a person feel comfortable no matter what emotion he has -- happy, sad, or anything else.

So how can a person feel comfortable in being unhappy? Many people look at the concept of comfort and happiness in the same way that they look at material wealth -- "they are happier than I am, so I must strive more to be as happy as they are". We are hence predisposed to feel a certain way -- though in fact, neither the happy nor the unhappy person can completely control their feelings. Happy people cannot permanently retain happiness, and unhappy people cannot always repel what is making them unhappy.

When practicing mindfulness, a person may feel sad -- then the emotion transitions to anger or frustration because he cannot keep a calm and peaceful mind. Here, anger, frustration, and the inability to meditate are just reactions to the initial emotion -- sadness. So here is the question -- how does sadness make you feel?

Nine times out of ten, your answer is the obvious -- sadness. But this is not always correct. The emotion of sadness is just our idea of what a sad event or memory makes us feel. It is how we *think* it is, rather than how it *actually* is. The practitioner might insist -- "no, it really is making me feel sad!"

Then here is the next question -- where is this sadness springing from? Most of us would answer something like "everywhere", or "in the core of my being", or "deep within my mind". In fact, this is quite a difficult question to answer since sadness is felt most when our thoughts are colored by it, and we all know about the intangible nature of thoughts.

Try sitting in a quiet room, and mentally scanning your body from top to bottom. At each part, try feeling for the sadness, frustration, or whatever emotional hindrance you are having. You might have the sensation of locating a "center" of the sadness in a specific part of the body (most likely one that is directly connected to the events that caused the sadness). Then again, as you try to focus on that part, you might find that the location shifts into someplace else. Such a fleeting and ever-moving sensation can be hard to study. Another problem is that this is just one part in "identifying" the sadness -- in order to know something, you must also recognize its size, shape, etc.

Again, this is a tough call. Depending on the person, sadness and its associated emotions can be widespread or constricted, heavy or light. It is like a shadow. Try it for yourself -- devote a few minutes right now to find the center of the sadness, along with its different properties.

As you go through this exercise, you might find another aspect of this elusive sadness -- aside from being a fleeting, ever moving "entity", sadness also seems to weaken the more you focus on it. Trick? No, it's not -- this is a real property of emotions that mindfulness practitioners need to understand completely. Emotions, no matter how intense they may be, can be dampened simply by casting the light of awareness on them. The more you dive into the nature of your sadness, the more it shrinks.

Again, both mindfulness and meditation are meant to

increase awareness -- not as some forms of esoteric morphine meant to block out our pain points. The masters of these arts do not block out pain, not even those mountaintop monks. Instead, they are able to focus their awareness on the pain, sadness, regret, anger, etc. Through this awareness, they are able to live in relative comfort with whatever emotional baggage they have, secure in the fact that they are aware of the properties of these emotions.

Right now you must be thinking how difficult this approach may be, and it's true it's neither quick nor easy. Neither will achieving this level of awareness render you immune to attacks of unpleasant emotions. However, this experience is sure to teach you a lot of lessons, in the end allowing you to see the original emotion for what it really is -- intangible aspects of your personality that you have to accept with awareness. Shutting them out and resisting them only serves to give them more importance, allowing them to do the tasks they have set out to do (i.e., ruin your practice and your day).

'

Chapter X: Curiosity at Different Levels

Different people will have different approaches to the study of mindfulness, but each one has some sort of curiosity that will fuel his practice. It may be a bullish curiosity, the type that tries to learn everything all at once. These are the people who seek progress to a fault, and cannot be bothered to look at the minute things that happen in the practice. Needless to say, they usually miss the important parts that would have pointed to the next level of advancement.

On the other end of the spectrum are those who are too patient (again to a fault). These are like students who just let the instructors carry along with the lesson, trailing every step of the way. They usually lack initiative, and as such, progress can be painfully slow. Whereas the earlier example sets his eyes too much on the future without focusing on the wonders of the present, this one sits back and focuses on the present without thinking about the future in the least bit.

Mindfulness is a science inasmuch as an art form, and the study also benefits from the same attributes that allows one to progress in these two fields. These include a form of gentle curiosity, as well as a tempered initiative. As mentioned earlier, a common mistake in the process of mindfulness is when the practitioner attempts to find some kind of epiphany such as those seen in the movies. This makes one restless, finally prompting him to ditch the practice altogether.

In mindfulness, the journey and its goal are one and the same thing. The moment you attempt the process of sitting down and being aware (or going through motions of life *while* being aware, as you will see in the latter half of this book), then you are immediately achieving one of the goals of mindfulness -- the practice itself. Your motions -- how fast or slow you go through things, included -- directly and immediately affect what kind of mindfulness practice you have. Go too fast, and you cannot focus on the right things. Go too slow, and you grow stagnant.

Just like in any other science and art form, the best way to approach progress in mindfulness is "gentle curiosity". It is the process of carefully turning every stone until you gain intuitive knowledge and awareness of where you are at. When you are through, you can proceed to a different focus -- be it a specific event, idea, etc. Each and every thought that passes through the mind is unique and deserves careful study.

"Gentle curiosity" is a concept that also demands patient interest, the type that stays attentive even as it passively lets things unfold. Think of yourself as an entomologist sitting at your yard, watching the different species crawl across your backyard. While it's true that you might have seen some of them, it would not be right to simply idle around -- you will never know when a new and interesting one comes your way.

Chapter XI: Mindfulness in Research

To wrap up the first part of this book, it would only be proper to examine the different scientific evidence that point to the efficiency of mindfulness. These different studies will reinforce the different points we had made throughout this entire chapter.

Mindfulness practitioners activate the same area of the brain involved in the feeling of happiness. We have already established that mindfulness per se does not make you happier -- it makes you more "content" with your current state, which inches you on the road towards that elusive bliss. Scientifically, this is done by activating the front-left side of the brain during the practice -- the same area of the brain that lights up when you feel good.

On the other hand, a person deeply involved in anxious thoughts creates more activity at the brain's right side. The neuroscientists from the University of Wisconsin found in their studies that after only eight weeks of continuous mindfulness practice, the mind of the participants had a significant shift in activity from right to left.

Mindfulness reduces the impact of negative emotions. Another set of neuroscientists -- this time from the UCLA -- have found that people involved in mindfulness practice experience a reduced intensity of negative emotions. The process of labeling these emotions and cultivating awareness of them (as we have discussed earlier) does the trick.

Mindfulness counteracts the physical attributes of stress. That feeling of untangling emotions during mindfulness practice does not simply dwell in the mind -- it is also manifested physically. Stress evokes symptoms such as increased cholesterol levels, blood pressure, and even instances of stroke, hypertension, and heart disease. In contrast, the "relaxation response" caused by mindfulness eases the heart rate, blood pressure, breathing rate, and even oxygen consumption. Even the immune system is boosted, protecting the person from disease and increasing his overall well-being.

Mindfulness knocks back anxiety. A study conducted at the University of Massachusetts Medical School has verified that generalized anxiety disorder can be cured by mindfulness. An astonishing 90% of the participants in this study documented a significant reduction in feelings of anxiety and depression, after eight weeks of the practice. A follow-up made three years after the initial study verified that these improvements can be maintained for the long run.

Mindfulness and meditation jointly help reshape the brain -- literally. "Old dogs can't learn new tricks" is a common adage, but what if you can change the brain itself to accommodate new tricks? University of Montreal researchers verified that the brains of people who practice daily mindfulness in conjunction with a more formal meditation regimen have an increased development in the areas dedicated to pain and emotion regulation. The area becomes thicker, which directly lowers pain sensitivity. This field -- neuroplasticity -- is only being thoroughly studied in the modern times.

Mindfulness kicks away depression better than medications. Using a randomized control study, researchers have confirmed that using mindfulness-based approaches can be better than medication in preventing relapse in depression-stricken patients. In only half a year, 75% of the practitioners were completely weaned off their medications, with less fear of relapse. Verbatim comments also reported an increased quality of life over those still taking their medications.

Mindfulness is dermatologist approved. Treating skin diseases would perhaps be one of the last applications for mindfulness that you can think of. However, a Professor of Medicine from the University of Massachusetts Medical School had confirmed through research that mindfulness can be instrumental in healing psoriasis. This disease itself has a strong link to psychological stress. The skin of those practicing mindfulness cleared at about 4 times faster than non-practitioner.

Mindfulness is OB-GYN approved. This is even lower down the charts of common mindfulness applications. However, an Oxford University study took 274 healthy women between ages 18 and 40, and found that among the sample group, those who were exposed to the most stress were having the most difficulty in conceiving. The team's research head had suggested using mindfulness and meditation to counteract this -- with much success.

Mindfulness is sleep friendly. Mindfulness has been acclaimed by researchers from the University of Massachusetts Medical School as an effective way to approach sleep. More than half of the insomniacs participating in the study reported significant improvements. Around 91% of them either reduced or totally stopped their doses. Neuroscientists from the Stanford Medical Center also concluded that a mere six weeks of mindfulness can help a person sleep in about half the time he is used to.

Mindfulness is for beating deadlines. Mindfulness is often seen as the antithesis of being "primed for war". The latter is often the attitude one takes when finishing a project as the deadline approaches. However, several studies on the process have found that subjects who practiced mindfulness after just four days are better able to keep mental attention for a longer amount of time. This extends to tasks that are high-stress and time-bound. All the cognitive tests used in the study showed an improvement for the mindfulness group.

It is very important to note that while these studies are all made by different groups of scientists, all of them have one thing in common -- they are all conducted after the participants have created a meaningful mindfulness practice. This is not just the participants doing things once or twice. This underscored the importance of repetition in your practice. Just like the any physical regimen (a new sport or an exercise), mindfulness must be done consistently in order for it to take effect. Just as how muscles are developed by exercise, new synaptic pathways (means for information to efficiently get from one neuron to another) are successfully created with the repetition of mindfulness.

This is why mindfulness should as much be a part of your life as bathing, brushing your teeth, and similar activities are.

PART 4:

The Practice

Chapter XII: Living Mindfully

We're going to start this with a simple but difficult exercise. Simple because the steps are easy to do: they don't take much thought and they aren't physically demanding. But difficult because they go against everything you have ever been trained to do in your adult life. Ready?

Starting by removing all of the distractions around you; put that smartphone or tablet on silent (not vibrate) and move it or turn it over so you can't see the screen or better yet, move it to another room or turn it off altogether. Turn off the television or the music player. Make sure the cats, dogs and kiddos are fed or sleeping or under the care of another adult.

Now, close your eyes and concentrate on what's happening outside your building. Listen to the sounds of the traffic, the people, or the nature outside. Are the birds chirping? Are crickets buzzing? Has someone's dog gotten annoyed at the stars yet again and decided to let the entire neighborhood know about it? When you're ready, think about what's happening in the next room. Can you hear the coffee machine running? Is the air conditioner or the heater clicked on? When you're ready again, concentrate on what's happening in the room that you are in. Think about the sounds around you. The smell of your perfume or cologne. How your feet are laying and whether they are comfortable. What are you doing with your hands right now? Are you hungry? Are you relaxed or tense? Try tightening up your entire body, every muscle in your power, and count to ten. Now, release every muscle slowly, starting from your feet and hands and working your way slowly to your core.

Now we're going to breath

Take in a deep breath and hold it. Feel your lungs fill up. Feel your chest expand and your stomach lower as your shoulders rise. Slowly exhale. Feel the breath rush past your lips.

Say to yourself "I am exhaling. I am exhaling."

Again. Deep breath in. "I am inhaling. I am inhaling."

And exhale. "I am exhaling. I am exhaling."

When you're ready, open your eyes.

That is an example of living in the moment. When the only thoughts, the only desires and the only purpose of your being is to understand where you are, what you're doing and how you're feeling. More than that, it's listening to yourself. What is your body telling you?

Obviously, you can't walk around with your eyes closed trying to concentrate on everything intensely all the time. That's what this book is about. Learning how to bring yourself back into the moment. Learning who you are in this moment and, most importantly, believing in who you are in this moment.

Chapter XIII: Be Aware

Mind what You Put into Your Body

Living mindfully means bringing yourself to a full sense of awareness about you and your body. And if you've been living the same busy lifestyle as so many others, chances are you haven't really given much thought to the types of fuel you've been living on.

This isn't going to be some sermon on how you should be living like a vegan or cutting out red meat or restricting your carbohydrate access. But the food you eat should be nourishing. Read the packaging carefully to see what vitamins and minerals each is providing you, care less about calories and more about chemicals and avoid as many as you can and put together a meal that can meet the energy demands of your lifestyle. There are several websites and smartphone apps that can help you determine what each food is providing you with. Use these to your advantage to create a diet that will nourish you, not just fill you up.

Of course, some junk foods, treats, desserts and even drinks may still find themselves lingering around your kitchen. And that's okay in moderation. This isn't about condemning particular food groups, or about judging you for not being the healthiest person on the block.

Rather, this is to make you aware of the food you eat

and aware of the way the food fuels your body.

Eat and Drink Slowly

If you're like most busy professionals, breakfast is something of a blur, lunch is probably nonexistent and supper is a blend of storytelling, last minute cleaning, and checking on tasks still left over from work. It's time to stop all of that. Eating mindfully means savoring each bite. Relishing every sip. Appreciating every breath you hold to swallow and the feeling of satisfaction as the food makes its journey down your esophagus. It means taking the time to really enjoy your meal and the nourishment that it is bringing to you. Additionally, listen to your body. Stop eating once your body is satisfied and nourished. No more worrying about whether or not you've cleaned your plate. No more eating so much food you feel sick and bloated.

Stay in the moment with each bite. Your body will feel better for it and so will you. Feel the textures bump against your tongue. Breathe in deep right before you take a bite and savor the aroma of each ingredient. Having a burger? Close your eyes and concentrate on each and every topping: the way the pickles dance against the beef. The way the cheese sticks briefly to the roof of your mouth. The way the buttered roll crunches slightly when you bite down into it. The way the acid in the mustard teases at your senses and sets the nerves at the back of your tongue on fire. Savor every moment of your bite.

Take Your Day One Step at a Time

Multitasking is a wonderful and often desirable skill to have. However, without proper discipline, multitasking can quickly take over your life. When was the last time you sat down to eat and just ate? When was the last time you did anything without also either thinking about the past or planning out a bit of the future? Ever take a shower in the morning and not try to also map out your day? Ever take a bath at night and not think about everything you tried to do that day? To live mindfully means that while you are brewing yourself a cup of coffee, for that moment, that is all you are doing. No running to grab the paper real quick, no stepping over the cat to shove some bread into the toaster, and no sorting out the day's to-do list in your head as you stir in the creamer.

Just brew the coffee.

Have you ever seen a coffee commercial on television before? Are the people in the commercial ever enjoying their coffee while they run around, dodging each other's briefcases and tossing kisses at their children? No. In those moments of chaos and pandemonium, it's hard to even recognize what good can come from a cup of coffee.

But then the moment comes. The music slows down. The steam wafting up from the cup of coffee tickles the person's nostrils, and he or she smiles and closes his or her eyes. Then, the sip. They hold the coffee in their mouth for a moment, then swallow and lick their lips.

That is the epitome of mindful living.

Once you've finished brewing the coffee, move on to the next task, whatever that may be.

Move Slowly and Deliberately

Rushing through the task at hand is a sign of multitasking: you're trying to hurry so you can get to doing something else. For example, maybe you're speeding on the drive home so you can hurry up and get supper started. Rushing through one task in hopes of starting another task isn't staying in the moment. It's allowing the future to try to take over your thoughts again, and bring with it anxiety and stress.

Stick with one thing at a time, and give it your full attention. Make sure every second you spend on that activity is planned and deliberate. Doing this will help you to keep from rushing and possibly making mistakes.

During that drive home, try to monitor your breathing. Stuck at a red light? Rather than tapping your fingers anxiously awaiting the green signal to carry about your trip, try taking in a deep breath and thinking about how comfortable your seat is. Take a look around you and try wishing each person also stopped at the light a nice day. Concentrate on how the steering wheel feels gripped between your fingers. How the gum you're chewing feels as you gnash your teeth.

Take in each moment of the drive. Make each moment purposeful and meaningful, and you will find the drive to be more enjoyable.

Chapter XIV: Meditation

Turn Chores into Opportunities
to Meditate

A lot of times, while I am talking to people about the benefits of mindfulness, the answer I receive is usually they don't have time to meditate. And it's probably true, a lot of us don't have 10, 20 or 60 minutes to spare everyday just to meditate. But meditating is such a large part of living mindfully.

Think about the short meditation I walked you through earlier in this chapter. Meditation helps ground our thoughts and bring them into the present. It helps silence the distractions and allows us to listen to our bodies in order for us to concentrate in the moment and define our thoughts, our feelings and our emotions right then and there, without bias from the past and without worry about the future.

So, how does a busy person such as yourself find time to meditate?

First, take a look around your house. More specifically, take a look at those chores no one likes to do.

Cooking, vacuuming, laundry: whatever chore in your household you normally do but try to speed through because you don't like to do it. That is the perfect chore to turn into an opportunity to meditate.

Next time you're at the sink washing dishes, bring your

entire self into the moment and concentrate on each of your thoughts. Calm your breathing and ground yourself. Don't rush through those dishes, but rather give each dish your undivided attention. By the time you're finished, you will feel more energized, more present and more accomplished at how well the dishes turned out!

The next time you're giving your toddler a bath, concentrate on the sound of water filling up the bathtub. Take a deep breath and feel how warm the water is. Say to yourself: "I am giving my child a bath. I am giving my child a bath."

The beauty of this technique is that it can be done anywhere. At work pounding away on a keyboard? Breathe deeply and concentrate on the keys you're using. Meditate on how the chair feels against your back. How are your legs crossed beneath the desk? Sit up straight and pay attention to your posture. Obviously, if you work with heavy machinery or in a factory you can't run the risk of closing your eyes and meditating. But you can meditate during your lunch break, or while you're in the bathroom.

Meditation is a wonderfully versatile and flexible tool. All you need to make it work is a safe situation and a desire to ground yourself in the present moment. It doesn't require a lot of time or effort. All it requires is consistency and dedication.

Chapter XV: Loving Mindfully

Just when you think you might have a handle on living mindfully, someone else walks into the room and expects you to interact with him or her. The truth is most of us have someone in our lives that we love. Whether we are talking about the love between a parent and a child, a wife and her husband, or between siblings, love makes up a large part of everyone's life. A lot of what we do is in the name of love. Love can drive us to do many things, which, if not for love of that person, we might not ever dream of doing or might be too scared to try.

The type of love you experience depends on the nature of your relationship with the person. But in the end, all of your personal relationships will grow deeper and more fulfilling by approaching your relationship mindfully. In addition to the tips we covered in the first chapter, these tips will help you learn how to love mindfully.

When You're Talking to Someone, Be Present

Too many times, people allow machines to get in the way of their conversations. The television is on in the background, the computer screen is on. People are at work, talking on the phone, or carrying on two or three conversations at the same time. We live in a busy world and sadly, most of our conversations have become buttons for autopilot.

Someone will leave the room yelling over her shoulder "Love you" and be answered by someone whose eyes are still glued to their smartphone: "Love you too." Many of us don't even realize that our conversations are empty words, the meanings behind which have been lost in a sea of activity and agendas.

Now is the time to put an end to all of that. Concentrate on the words coming from his or her mouth. Watch his or her body language. Don't think about the last time you two had this same argument. While they are talking, don't think about how you're going to answer and don't try to formulate a response.

Listen to their words.

Watch their hand movements.

Look into their eyes and really see their eyes.

Even if this is the 53rd time your aging grandmother has told you this story about how she met your grandfather, absorb her words. Listen to how patient her voice is.

When it's your time to talk, choose your words carefully. Take a deep breath and ground yourself in the moment and talk. Listen to the words as they come out, feel the inflection in your voice.

This isn't about not interrupting the other person, or even about active listening. Both of those are important and both of those show your respect for someone. This is a more in depth level of conversation; one in which for that moment, all you are doing is conversing with the other person. Nothing else. Savor the conversation.

Be Compassionate

Compassion is a deep awareness that someone else— anyone else—is in some way suffering or hurting accompanied by the wish to help ease that hurt. Now, you might be thinking "okay, well if someone I love is hurt, of course I want to help" and that's great. But that's not always true.

When was the last time you were in the heat of an argument with someone you love and felt compassion for what he or she must be going through? When was the last time your child cried because of something you thought was mundane or unimportant and you dismissed his or her cries as a tantrum?

To be compassionate means to look deeper than how you believe you would react to a given situation and find the hurt feelings beneath someone's actions. The next time your toddler cries because you told her that ketchup just doesn't taste good on cereal, try to concentrate on what it must feel like to be told the one thing you want more than anything in the world won't be good. Think about what it must be like to want to be held and comforted only to be told that you shouldn't feel upset or hurt.

Come back to the person with a level of compassion and understanding that he or she is hurting and you want to help ease that hurt.

This is especially important when interacting with people you don't know, or with people you don't know very well. Society today has become desensitized to the needs and suffering of others. You'll find that offering compassion to someone else, no matter that person's plight, will help you develop a higher sense of awareness about yourself, your family, and your friends.

You don't have to agree with his or her actions to want to ease the hurt. And, thankfully, you don't have to put ketchup in your toddler's cereal to help him or her feel better.

Compassion is not the same as condoning a particular behavior, but it does sometimes require you to look past the behavior.

Be Grateful

While growing up, most of us were taught to always say "Please" and "Thank you." These were the pillars of manners. These simple phrases, along with a few others, would become the foundation of polite interaction with everyone in society: clients, employers, parents, siblings, classmates, coworkers, and partners. And because of their long-term, widespread use, many times people utter these phrases without a second thought.

I have even caught myself saying "Thank you" when the other person didn't do anything. I have often apologized when I didn't do anything that would require an apology. I've apologized for apologizing before.

Running these words on autopilot all the time has caused them to lose some of their meaning and people are getting away with simply muttering their way through the emotions. But they do nothing to truly define the level of gratitude many of us experience.

When your partner or spouse does something for you, be truly thankful for what he or she has just done. Take a moment to concentrate on the scope of that favor or surprise, big or small and what it must have take for him or her to accomplish such a task. Take a deep breath and be aware of how the emotions are flowing through your body right now. Are the muscles in your cheeks tugging at the corners of your mouth to bring it into a smile? Is your heart racing at the anticipation of the gift? Or can you breathe a sigh of relief at the sight of long awaited coffee?

Stop spitting out the phrase "thank you" without feeling truly grateful.

Take a moment to recognize and savor just how grateful you are, and what grateful feels like. Your relationship will be deeper and stronger for it.

Concentrate on Who You Are in the Relationship

So often, we spend so much time thinking about the other person in the relationship and what he or she means to us, we forget that we should be concentrating on who we are in the relationship. We think of all the things he or she does for us, all the things we wish he or she would do for us. Those annoying habits that get under our skin alongside those wonderful traits that make him or her perfect for you.

For those of you not in an intimate relationship, how often have you thought about the traits and characteristics you would like to find in a potential partner? And how much time have you thought about the traits and characteristics you possess that another person might be looking for in a partner? How do you make the relationship stronger? What do you bring to the relationship? What kind of partner or spouse are you?

These questions will bring you into the present, allowing

you to concentrate on the answers and, if you need to, work on areas so you like the answers.

Obviously, this section can lead to some negative feelings. So now may be a good time to take a break, take a breath and remember that this book is not about blaming or finding fault with anything. This is about recognizing your fears, emotions, anxieties and characteristics in a truthful and nonjudgmental way. The goal is not to make you feel bad about your lifestyle or about your relationships. On the contrary, the goal of this book is to make you more aware of your lifestyle so you can strengthen your relationships.

Know When Not to Check Your Phone

This might seem like it comes straight out of a guide for common sense. But all too often we see people trying to hold a conversation while they are checking their email, checking their social media accounts, or even while playing a game. And while there is nothing inherently wrong with this—in fact, most people would completely understand and probably do the same thing themselves—it allows the phone to be physically placed between you and a loved one. Children are forced to fight against a tablet or computer for your attention. Spouses are being told to hold onto their thoughts so their partners can finish a level of Angry Birds. As social beings, humans thrive on human touch and human interaction. Smartphone have their roles to play in connectivity, but the next time you go out to eat with the family, try leaving your smartphone in the car and see how much easier it is to be in the moment, enjoying your family, at the restaurant. You'll find the entire experience to be more enjoyable than before.

There is a time to check your smartphone, and there is a time to leave it be. Knowing the difference can mean the difference between enjoying time with your friends and loved ones or being rushed through your day feeling lonely and unappreciated.

Let Go of Control

Try as we might, we can't control everything. In fact, we can't control anything. All the lists, agendas, day planners, calendars—all these tools we use to try to predict and prepare for anything give us the illusion of control. But the truth of the matter is, we just can't control life. You can cook the perfect holiday dinner, but traffic may still interfere and make your relatives late, which causes the food to overcook and dry out, which leads to frustration.

We often think we have control, and we like it that way. So when something happens that reminds us we don't actually have anything under our control, we get frustrated, upset and angry. We might try to blame the person, the event, or even the situation, but the truth is the anger we feel is a symptom that we were not living in the moment, and we fear our loss of control.

Rather than tightening your grip over other people and their actions, or trying to control everything around you, start to loosen your grasp. The only person you can control is the same person who shares your mind. That's right: you.

When something happens that knocks your plans for a loop, take a deep breath and remind yourself you can't control what happened, but you can control how you react to what happened. You can choose to get angry, or you can choose to let it go. One of these choices will lead to anxiety and discomfort, and will probably contribute to others' bad moods as well. The other choice will lead to a heightened sense of awareness, a new level of problem solving, and a brighter outlook on the entire event.

The first step in figuring out who you are today is to accept your past. I know, I told you earlier that we were going to stop dwelling in the past. But by accepting your past, we aren't going to be dwelling. Rather, we are going to review your past, learn how each decision, each choice and every move helped shape the person you are today and let go of the regrets. We don't want to forget about the experience you had altogether, but rather we want to let go of the pain you feel when you remember that experience.

You see, the past is gone. Last year is gone. This morning is gone. And although the actions you took last year or this morning might still be influencing your day today, they are over. Languishing over the actions can't undo the action; no matter how hard we try. And because the past is made up of unchangeable moments, it doesn't deserve power over your life today.

Equally important to learning these various steps and tricks to living a new, mindful life is to understand that adapting mindful living won't happen overnight. Mindful living is a lifestyle. That is to say, it is a conglomeration of patterns, beliefs, values, and experiences that come together to help formulate your outlook on the world. You will likely make mistakes and slip back into your busy, autopilot life only to miss out on hours of your day. And that's okay. You must give yourself permission to make such mistakes.

If you do find that you've slipped backward, take a moment to bring yourself into the moment and concentrate on how you feel about the mistake. What are your thoughts about implementing mindful living again? Take a few deep breaths, and understand that mindful living means, by definition, never being placed on hold. It will always be available to you. So every attempt is just that, an attempt. A trial run. A practice session, if you will. And by giving yourself this permission in the moment, you strengthen your chances of getting better and better at it as you try and try again.

PART 5:

The Integration

Chapter XVI: The Tamed Horse

In many ways, mindfulness and meditation is like a martial art. This is one of the many reasons why the practice is inextricably linked to the latter when it comes to movie portrayals. That, and because most martial artists actually spend a significant amount of time doing both.

Like martial arts, the way you learn mindfulness depends a lot on the person who teaches you. Common enough is the picture of people sitting on tatami mats, backs straight and cross-legged, probably chanting some mantra or another. Then again, many a young monk-aspirant has been surprised after seeing his mentors spending almost the whole day walking in various places around the monastery. Walking *and* meditating at the same time. Inevitably, that's what the young monk would learn to emulate.

In the previous chapters, we have described the different ways to practice mindfulness in various life activities -- from something as mundane as eating and drinking to something as important as relationships. If you just read through all that without actually trying out any of the exercises (and committing to the actions implied in each chapter), you might start thinking about when you will read about the "magic" sitting pose that lets you transcend your limitations. Many of us

(Westerners, especially), have grown up believing this to be the "right" way of meditating. But as discussed during the first chapter, if this was to be the sole way of practicing mindfulness, then you would not be able to integrate it in your daily life.

A non-practitioner may find that the mindfulness practice can go to such extremes that one is even encouraged to stay mindful *through the night, while sleeping.* Yes, there is also such a thing as horizontal meditation, of the formal kind. Its use ranges from those needing to fall asleep, to those who are too ill to meditate upright. Falling asleep during horizontal meditation supposedly encourages a mindful sleep (though this is commonly taught to more advanced students -- it needs both a correct position and a right attitude of the mind). Practitioners of this form of mindfulness are supposed to be able to tell if they woke up on an in-breath or an out-breath -- a level of awareness unprecedented for the rest of us.

What does this tell us? This means that mindfulness can be literally injected into any form of activity, throughout the day. However, this brings another question. It is one thing to be involved in such an activity as, say, cross-stitching that your mind is focused only on it. You are mindful of each motion, as your focus on the activity acts in concert with your desire to maintain awareness. But how about more mundane things like walking? Doesn't such mindless activities invite all sorts of mindless thoughts?

It doesn't have to, but it often does, especially if one is still beginning. The way here, however, is to remove the connotation of walking as a "mindless" process. Even though it is automatic, the practitioner can use the very sensations that arise from walking -- the feeling of muscles pulling your leg, the ground as it rolls from your heels to your toes, the pressure as you lift your other foot -- as anchors of mindfulness. By giving your complete awareness to all these processes, walking takes center stage in the mind -- effortlessly crowding out any unproductive thoughts you might have.

This is a scientific concept, too -- no two things can occupy the same space at the same time. As the process of walking takes up your mind, awareness of it creates a space where other negative things cannot intrude in. Of course, this takes practice -- otherwise, what you will get is simply a repressive, hypnosis-like state.

At first, this concept might not seem to be an extraordinary revelation. After all, it is but natural for us to calm our minds by focusing it on something else. We listen to music when we are feeling down. We watch TV to help us forget about our problems. We seek the company of friends to help us resolve issues. If it is that simple, though, why do we only do it sporadically? The practice of mindful integration allows us to place this technique in the middle of our lives, living in it even as we perform varying activities. It allows us to discipline the mind as we train it to stay at one place at any given time. Remember that wild horse we mentioned as an example during the first part of this book? This is the time when you have already tamed it, enough so that it does not just stay in one place, but so that you can bring it to different points as needed.

Chapter XVII: Putting Mindfulness in Action

As you may have already experienced, staying mindful for extended periods of time requires consistent effort -- our natural tendency to mull over trivialities is just around the corner. However, many resources will push you to be as effortless as possible. Is it possible to maintain an *effortless* effort in your mindfulness practice?

When we pare it down, most of the effort we exert in the practice comes from remembering to notice when we are caught up in feelings, thoughts, or others that do not benefit us. From there, we try to redirect our attention back to a specific point of focus -- such as the activity at hand. This is why an easily noticeable sensation -- such as a firm grip or the taste of food -- is often touted as the best anchors of mindfulness. That way, the practitioner can readily redirect his attention.

For example, some activities have very particular sensations that we often take for granted, simply because we perform the too often. One such activity is brushing the teeth. No other activity produces the same stimuli that tooth-brushing makes, turning these sensations into particularly good anchors. You can focus on the sound of the brushing, on the bristles rubbing against your gums, on the smell of the toothbrush, or on the feeling of foam. It is advisable to choose only one among these sensations, so as not to run into the overwhelmed feeling we are keeping at bay. If we commit to it, there's a good chance that we can very easily maintain mindfulness throughout the entire activity.

When these principles are applied, the practitioner begins to soothe his mind from the things that pollute it. He gains calm and clarity, which in turn allows him to see into his own actions. He can understand why he thinks and acts the way he does. Patterns and tendencies come to the surface, and he regains the choice of conducting life as he wants -- not as external things dictate.

Chapter XVII:
Mindfulness in Public

Another common misconception is how people always associate the practice of mindfulness with solitude. In the previous part of this book, we had discussed different ways of applying mindfulness -- and surely many of those things are best done with other people.

Aside from the fact that our media bombards us with false images of mindfulness, many people are concerned that mindfulness can be extremely hard to achieve when around others. As social creatures, we are naturally focused to the words, feelings, and various nuances that other people have -- leaving us with little attention left to spend on mindfulness.

However, when was the last time you *really* listened to someone talking? Most of the time, it is not *their* words that distract us from mindfulness -- it is our own. We have so much going on in our minds, and we often worry about how to appropriately react to the other person even before they have finished speaking.

The proof that we can spare the mental cycles for mindfulness even when with others is in the fact that we unconsciously do this every day. Let's say that you are walking in a park with a friend, and you are having a conversation. Though walking is considered automatic, a certain degree of deliberate decision-making still applies to make sure you don't bump or trip over. That does not mean that you cannot converse well with your companion. Most likely, during this time, you are also thinking about a lot of things in the background.

As you see, the mere *intention* to be aware of your surroundings causes you to walk safely even while responding appropriately. If you *intend* to be mindful at this point, then you will be able to ease out all the distracting thoughts to continue with your practice. While this may not be easy to accomplish at first, it gets more and more refines the more you do it.

Mindfulness even helps people achieve a new level of companionship as they tend to create an atmosphere of togetherness with whoever they are at the moment. A mother may be "one" with her baby by being mindful around him. A friend may become more "present" around another friend, instead of having his mind wander to other thoughts at various moments. This is what it means to give someone your complete and undivided attention (and to return the favor once someone does so).

Chapter XIX:

The Time Factor and the Wobbly Lines

One of the main advantages of mindfulness over meditation is the fact that you do not need to take a chunk of time of your day just to continue your practice. All it requires of you is to train your mind to be ever-present in each action you take. This is a direct answer to critics of the practice who say that they don't have enough time to train the mind.

However, there is another advantage mindfulness has. Whereas meditation is only restricted to the time when you are sitting in practice, mindfulness can extend to the whole day. It is like a program running quietly in the background of your mind, optimizing the things you do. As we had mentioned before, this can even extend up to the time when you sleep. It would not matter if you are living a sedentary life as an office worker, or an active life as an athlete. Both can have the same benefits, even though they have almost no similarity in how they carry out the practice. As the old saying goes, each man has the same 24 hours in a day -- it will depend on him what he puts in those 24 hours. But why cram in stressing and unnecessary thoughts when you can optimize everything with less effort?

Another way that mindfulness bridges the constraints of time is in the way it links everyday into a cosmic dot-to-dot drawing. This illustrates how mindfulness is a lot more than a permanent mental exercise we strive to maintain every day. Imagine yourself trying to draw a straight line on paper -- without a ruler, even the most skilled hand could produce little wobbles as the tip of the pen goes from point A to point B. This is just like us going through day-to-day, dot-to-dot with a consciousness that may at times be wobbly -- even if we use conventional steps to train for efficiency.

One reason a hand produces a shaky line when arbitrarily drawing on paper is because it lacks anchors. This is one of the many roles that mindfulness plays. Imagine any dot-to-dot drawing and try making a straight line from one dot to another. Easy, right? You can do this forever until you create a finished work. It's all because of the anchors, which force us to focus on that single short line. Mindfulness, in the same way, forces us to anchor in our awareness of the present, allowing us to carry on throughout the rest of the day with minimal to no "wobbles" in our consciousness.

Chapter XX: Living in Excitement

Unless you have tried the process of mindfulness yourself, it might all seem like boring talk. However, the practice is potentially very exciting. When we think about it, some of the most boring moments of life turn out to be those moments when we are living life on autopilot. You may be commuting daily to work without noticing the events around you. You might be carrying out routine phone conversations without completely understanding the things the other person says.

On the contrary, the most exciting parts of life are those that put you in the moment, allowing you to deliberate your immediate action which you know will result in a tangible effect the next moment.

In the same vein, mindfulness puts you in that moment no matter how menial the activity. It allows you to turn each moment into miniature exciting events that add up into a better day. There are times when you will ask yourself -- where have I been for all my life? You would surely notice certain activities that you have been doing all your life, but you only now have been thoroughly "in". You might have walked down the same flight of stairs all your life, but only now have you noticed the peeling paint. Or you might have been riding the same bus for years, but only now have you seen how the driver looked like! New things always open up to the mindful person.

Chapter XXI: Aversion and Desire

One of the things that constantly color our lives -- aside from the errant thoughts scurrying about -- are the judgments we make every day. And we do not mean judgments as in strategic decisions -- we mean those times when we judge the value of things, people, etc. Eventually, these lead us to the concept of like and dislike. These two things are ever-present and carry an important role (if sometimes unrecognized) in integrating our mindfulness practice into daily life.

Let's say you have been invited to dinner at the house of a new friend. This friend turned out to be vegetarian, and you are a true-blood carnivore. You could barely hide your dismay as you are served a stew with broccoli and carrots that you disliked the most. Now, this may not be really you -- but you could readily see how you would have reacted in this situation. Just how will you be focusing on your awareness of the matter at hand when you dislike the sensory inputs you are getting? It's one thing to deal with strong negative emotion, but it's another to be mindful of unpleasantness happening *in the same moment* you are in. Wouldn't it be better to seek a diversion instead?

Believe it or not, there are actually some monasteries that serve the food that the monks hated the most. You could say they were being trained in a tough-love kind of way, but there's a different story behind it. The original idea was to make sure that the monks do not indulge in the food they eat -- as indulgence is a pleasure that can counteract mindfulness. It also has the indirect effect of making each monk question exactly why they hated that certain food.

When many of us are asked why we hate the things we do, we can reply by describing the taste, texture, color, aroma, etc. There are times, however, when we simply dislike them without being able to put a finger on any specific quality. We just assume that we dislike things and like others.

One of the reasons for this is the inherent judgmental mind of humans, along with our tendency to think of things as ideas. More often than not, we dislike things because of our *ideas* of the attributes of these things, instead of direct and mindful *experience* of the same. We dislike vegetables because they are vegetables, even though not all of them look or taste the same. We hate hard work because of the idea of difficulty, instead of the fulfilling and rewarding experience it may hide. We may dislike people for their perceived attitude or status, without actually *experiencing* being in their company for a long time. The exact opposite may also be true, for everything -- we may like a certain person, thing, or experience until we are finally aware of the consequences or implications of our decisions.

Needless to say, mindfulness helps us keep a handle on this see-saw of aversion and desire. Once we are aware of the experiential nature of things, we are able to edge out the suggestions of (possible unfounded) ideas from our subconscious. We start paying closer attention to things as soon as the cover of like and dislike disappears. We understand why we tend to react in certain ways to certain stimuli. Unhealthy obsessions also fade out after some time -- no wonder that "mindful eating" has also been (unjustly) isolated and turned into one of the many diet fads floating around!

Chapter XXII: Obsession and Anger

While we are on the subject of obsession, there is another aspect to it that we need to discuss. Most of us do not realize (not until we practice mindfulness, at least) how much obsession is linked to anger, and how much this is linked to how we integrate the practice of awareness in our daily lives.

For our purposes, we will consider "obsessions" to be anything we want dearly -- which is commonly almost everything we like at all. For example, we are often obsessed with doing things right, and doing things fast. When something goes wrong or if there's an unexpected hold up, we are irritated. If everything goes south and if things start taking forever, we panic -- then flare up.

Simply put, when we do not get what we want, we commonly react with frustration. This seems to be inevitable. And yet, few have personally witnessed just how hard it is to fluster a trained monk or a yogi. How can they maintain their mindful attitude in the midst of stressors like these?

To almost all of us, anger, frustration, and its ilk are all natural responses. We know this, and yet we often do not admit it. At the back of our minds, we almost always shun anger, thinking it inappropriate. Of course, we can't -- and that obsession to remove something inevitable causes only more anger and frustration, feeding a vicious cycle.

One of the first things we must then realize is that awareness also calls for the acceptance of the inevitable. Just as we examine negative emotions as well as our likes and dislikes, we should also examine immediate and instinctive reactions such as anger. We must *accept* it, instead of pushing it away. All that talk we had earlier about resistance and acceptance come into play once more. When something comes up that does not go according to plan, it is important that we *anticipate* anger as a possible response -- whether we really go that way is dictated by our emotional fortitude, but at least we should recognize that route.

We should also be aware of the follow-through -- this usually comes in the form of sadness or guilt (the latter usually stemming from the fact that we think we shouldn't have been angry). Petty anger usually has a short lifespan, and its intense momentum may fade out quickly. Sadness, however, stays for a longer term. Despite this, the less intense reactions accompanying sadness allows the trained and aware mind to understand it better. Once the entire entourage of thoughts and emotions have passed under his scrutiny, the mindful person usually chalks what he has gleaned up to experience on the way to building a better response to anger and frustrations.

See, the mind of the monk or the yogi is not immune to bouts of anger or frustration, just like the rest of us. He feels these impulses as well. It is just that his mind is trained through mindfulness to contain these emotions, allowing him to process the feeling completely without letting it out in a harmful way. The anger is dissipated, the sadness and its accompanying aftermath is taken care of, and we are left with the image of the immovable and unflustered master of the mind. We, too, can achieve this with constant practice as we get rid of obsessions while dealing with its adverse reactions.

Chapter XXIII: Competitiveness

Man is inherently competitive, and we strive to perform to the best of our ability when the situation demands it. How many times have you gone in full competitive mode and felt good about yourself? There are times when you do not even need to win -- just the thought of giving things your best shot is enough to elicit a pleasant feeling. The feeling of being "in the zone" is often enough to beat out our self-criticism. A sense of focus, confidence, and unyielding will may prevail. Come to think of it, it rarely matters if the competition was grueling -- there is an effortless aura that surrounds it. This is the same quality that is true for mindfulness.

If you watch sports, you will see how many athletes spend a great amount of time trying to stay "in the zone". Sometimes, they slip out of it -- only to regain their footing. Once they have found it, they are at their peak and their focus seems indestructible. This is a focus that is directed inward -- a focus that can block out everything that can distract them from their game. The great athletes have found a way to balance an awareness of their own movement and physical state as well as that of the ever-changing surroundings. Even their effort is finely-tuned, allowing for a natural sustenance that hides the power behind the movements. Effortless and graceful movements mask the calculated and focused motion. This gives the illusion that even though they are using less effort than anyone else, they are performing much better. Again, all of these discussed traits are those shared with the practice of mindfulness.

Many of these people have a natural talent for their sport, but a lot can still be learned from the way these individuals apply their effort. Try viewing the super-slow motion shot of a race, such as a 100-meter sprint. This is the type of video that shows everything, from the facial expressions to the movement of the muscles as they propel the body forward. Notice the faces of those who are at the front. More often than not, they are the most composed and relaxed of the bunch. Their cheeks even wave up and down and side to side as they run. Now, notice those who are trailing -- those who are doing all the chasing. Usually, they have the grimaced faces as they realize that the race is quickly getting away from them. These runners tighten up and attempt to compensate with more effort, losing the balance of body and mind that is so evident in the frontliners.

This speaks much about the way mindfulness should be integrated into everyday life. How much effort do you apply in your practice? Do you chase both time and progress and tighten up as you go? This could also speak for the activities that are connected to mindfulness -- even the most menial ones such as pulling back the drapes, sweeping the floor, and getting up for coffee. Try assessing yourself as you do your tasks and check if you are like the trailing runners.

Because mindfulness just "rides" on top of your daily

activities, the level of effort you apply to even the simplest things will carry over into your mindfulness. Many people say that modern life is like a competition, but this does not mean that you have to approach every single process with a fighting spirit. Not only is this exhausting, it also undermines the role the calm mind plays in daily tasks.

As proven by a mindful experience, there is no separation between mind and body. A mindful person can hence seamlessly integrate presence of mind into his presence of body. This is done by possessing mental focus just as physical focus is achieved. It is also when ease of mind is paralleled by ease of body. This sounds really obvious, but how often do we really apply them? This far into your mindfulness practice, you might still have an uptight body even when your mind claims to be calm. This sets off a very unhealthy competition between body and mind, offsetting the balance and radically reducing any benefit you may have from mindfulness. Until this balance comes naturally, it will be difficult for one to consider his practice to be fully integrated.

It really does not matter if you are aiming to capitalize on mindfulness for a specific purpose such as pain management, mental endurance, or your ability to work under pressure. All of those factors rely on a mind that works in harmony with the body -- and none of them call for an undue tensing or exertion. A present, alert, and focused mind is good, but it causes stress unless it can also produce a sense of ease and relaxation -- much like the great athletes. And like the greats, the only way to train this delicate balance is thorough and devoted practice.

Chapter XXIV: At the End of the Day

Earlier, we had mentioned in passing about a particularly unique meditation form that lasts even while you sleep. We will not be able to discuss that here, but we *will* talk about how to use mindfulness for that activity that seems to be more and more elusive as we grow older -- sleep.

Many people call the inability to sleep "insomnia". This might not always be correct, however -- if it happens every once in a while, then it's better called "being human". We have all experienced this at some point or another -- that time when the floodgates of thought and imagination are suddenly let loose as soon as your head hits the pillow. If we are to integrate mindfulness at every point of our lives, the last moments of wakefulness should not be an exception.

As we had discussed early on in this book, most of these thoughts are background noise that are almost always there throughout the rest of the day. The trained and mindful mind can learn to examine and curb these thoughts, but they often run amok just as your grip on daytime consciousness slips.

The inability to sleep causes the person to exert more undue effort -- as discussed in the previous chapter. This can produce even more tension, which ultimately makes it harder for you to control the thoughts. This feeds a vicious cycle! Furthermore, it affects your waking performance and creates a chain reaction for the better part of the day.

Things can even be made worse when we are met with a disturbance just at the point we have reached the folds of elusive sleep. Someone may knock on the door, a loud sound may come from the neighbors, someone may call, or you may suddenly remember an important thing you *should* have done just before you hit the sack.

Remember the metaphor of the wild horse we had used far earlier in this book? This is, again, your mind -- except that now it is tired from having to work all day. He would very much like to lie down -- but his master wouldn't let him.

Old habits die hard, and even the best mindfulness practitioners sometimes slip into attempts to *force* the mind into submission while trying to sleep. You will run into this tendency several times more as you go on. Forcing the mind -- or resisting the thoughts -- come in lots of different flavors. The most common is the active attempt to clear the mind by banishing each thought as it comes in. This is extremely frustrating and not the least bit effective. Then there is also the passive method, which is to mindlessly follow our spontaneous train of thoughts. These can take us into and around issues that plague us during the day, forcing us to confront minute and ultimately insignificant details with an unnoticed urgency. Somehow, entertaining these thoughts lead us further down the rabbit hole and away from sleep.

So what to do with this errant horse? We're going back to the extreme basics of mindfulness -- simply let go, loosen the ropes from the horse's neck. You have to learn to recognize which effort of resistance you are applying, and take steps against it. Step back from your thoughts, neither confronting nor entertaining them. This removes the sense of urgency and the stress from resisting, therefore relaxing your mind.

In your study of mindfulness, you might find that there can be a lot of different meditative techniques claimed to help you fall asleep. Some of these are taken from formal meditation practices, such as visualization and the use of mantras. Several of them are actually effective -- provided you are able to practice them correctly. The problem with most of these approaches is the fact that they leave little to no room for the fact that the mind is weak as it prepares for sleep. Our senses and attention start to slow down, which may leave us unable to practice anything further than basic mindfulness. Stepping back from the thoughts is *very* effective since it uses the least mental energy while also allowing the mind to settle to its "base state" of calm.

Once you have made it up to this point, you are well covered from the start right up to the end of every day.

Conclusion

Thank you again for taking the time to read this book!

I hope this book was able to help you to be present in mind as well as body in each and every moment.

The next step is to take action on the steps provided and apply them into your daily life.

If you have enjoyed this book, please be sure to leave a review on amazon to let us know how we are doing so we can continue to bring you quality ebooks.

Thank you!

Preview Of "Mindfulness: a Practical Guide on Mindfulness for Beginners"

What would really make you happier? Finding the right person or improving our relationship. Getting that promotion or building a stronger career. Money in the bank or the mortgage paid off. The list can go on. Yet even when we get the things we think we want, there is still the sensation that something is missing. The things we believe we need don't always help us in the way we expect.

Sometimes we can be so busy managing life that we are not experiencing it or not experiencing ourselves and the world around us. When we are not aware of the natural elements of life through our own senses, we slip into autopilot.

Mindfulness can help us to improve our physical and mental wellbeing by helping us to improve our awareness of ourselves and our surroundings. As a tradition, mindfulness has deep roots, stretching back to thousands of years into the timeless wisdom of the East. Scholars have detailed how mindfulness practices can be used as a way to wisdom while people from the world of sport, business and government today adopt mindfulness as part of their strategies for success.

There is a simpler and practical way to learn to live through mindfulness. This is the practice of mindfulness in our daily lives. This requires no elaborate courses or travel or even setting aside a great amount of time outside of our ordinary activities. Doing so can bring fresh discoveries by turning simple tasks into activities from which we get new experiences and help us to learn to live with the flow of thoughts and events which we take for granted.

Many beginners of mindfulness start with morning exercises for a few minutes which bring about deeper peace through greater awareness and many are very pleased with the results. But to learn how to live mindfully is to move into a way of life in which the same techniques can improve our lives in other areas. This is not as difficult as it sounds.

In the chapters which follow you will see how mindfulness can change the way we go through our days, do our work, build our relationships and develop an awareness of the world around us. Mindfulness itself is not a technique which involves any change. It is, in fact, the opposite, it is an approach used to deepen our own awareness. But that in itself promotes wellbeing and helps us to make changes in how we live.

Mindfulness is something we can practice with increasing skill but it is not something which we can ever exhaust. Wherever we are or whatever we are doing, we can turn to mindfulness, whether we are beginners or more experienced.

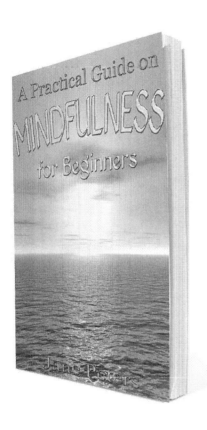

If you want to check out the rest of "Mindfulness: a Practical Guide on Mindfulness for Beginners"

go to: http://amzn.to/1Rs7pog

Made in the USA
Middletown, DE
04 November 2018